Sara is a native of the west country having spent her early years in Weston Super Mare. She left school at the age of 16 working as an office administrator. She married a RAF serviceman in 1976 then living in various parts of the country, returning to Locking village on the outskirts of Weston-super-Mare in 1988. Her passion for poetry started at the age of 20 when sadly her father passed away. She loves reading romantic, crime and true story novels. She is blessed with 18 grandchildren with an age range of four the youngest twins to a 21-year-old grandson. She loves writing about real life and experiences and will always want to help anyone in need.

I dedicate this book to my granddaughter, Chloe, who sadly died in 2004

My late sister, Angie, who also wrote poems and we used to dream of publishing a book of poetry

My dear friend, Sue, a wonderful friend who sadly departed this world too soon. I know you will be looking down from heaven and smiling as you always loved my poems.

Sara Angell

LIFE AS I SEE IT

AUSTIN MACAULEY PUBLISHERS™

LONDON • CAMBRIDGE • NEW YORK • SHARJAH

A CIP catalogue record for this title is available from the British Library.

ISBN 9781398446533 (Paperback)
ISBN 9781398446540 (ePub e-book)

www.austinmacauley.com

First Published 2022
Austin Macauley Publishers Ltd®
1 Canada Square
Canary Wharf
London
E14 5AA

My heartfelt thanks to Lesley Lacey for creating the necessary files for my publishers and not to forgetting the wonderful encouragement I've received from so many friends and family.

This morning I was watching two seagulls on a distant rooftop and wondered if like humans one was a husband and the other his wife.

As the male strutted back and forth across the slates, I imagined he was muttering, "Give it a rest, woman, with your nagging. I just want an easy life."

"We have achieved many things this week; lots of jobs done on your to-do list as well as flying miles travelling from Brighton to Burnham-on-Sea."

Before any of you that reads this little ode and thinks that I have finally lost the plot, my bird watching moment for some reason tickled me.

Try never to end a day on a quarrel, tell those who matter to you that you love them before you close your eyes in sleep.

For should the morning dawn without them, the lack of those three little words being spoken what bitter tears you will weep.

It is human nature to have disagreements. Why, life would be a little boring if we never had falling out.

We don't always have to apologise but even when we are disgruntled with each other, stay close for that's what love is about.

Borne Out of Love

When you lay in your bed in the quiet of the night
look up at the sky see the moon glowing so bright
A new star has been born twinkling now with God up above
her spirit left this earth surrounded by love
I know that your hurt goes deep down inside for I was
privileged to be with you right there by your side
There are no words that can express what I feel I just know
that in time, love will help you to heal
I have always been proud of you never more so than now for
when I prayed for strength, it was you who showed me how
It's unique it's a blessing this emotion we have for each other
there is no sweeter love than the love of a mother
Time really does help I know this to be true, your heart will
again be at peace for I believe in you
God needs an angel and though he saw the tears you cried he
chose your little girl to journey to the other side
She lived to know your love and your gentle touch she knows
you wanted to keep her so very much
She felt how hard you fought for her to exist, the courage of a
mother such a wonderful gift
On the days when your heart is so heavy with pain just close
your eyes and you will be able to see her again
Remember her tiny hand that you held for such a short while
try to picture her face wreathed in a smile
I can only imagine the emptiness your arms still feel such a
short time to cherish it seems almost surreal

Bittersweet memories that time will never erase wherever life takes us you will remember these days

Promise yourself on the days that you feel sad to take comfort from the brief time together that you had

Whatever you do or wherever you are, you are being watched over always by your own special star.

Please don't look down on me huddled in the shop doorway,
I have a story to tell that you do not know
Once like you I had a job, dressed smartly had a loving family
and a home where I could go
That elderly man on the street corner what happened to him
still reduces me to tears it's just not right
Last month a group of lads thought it was fun to kick his dog
and taunt him to stand up they were looking for a fight
Yet yesterday when only a few kind souls stopped and gave
him a coffee and dropped some coins into his hat
I watched him go into the butchers and buy scraps for his
faithful companion, nothing for himself, such love is that
On the seafront yesterday the wind was fierce and there
seemed no shelter anywhere to escape from the bitter cold
I felt for the young woman whose scarf blew away yet she
didn't see how wet the blanket was that I was trying to fold
I in my current circumstances don't know what the answer is
for the homeless situation in any given town or city
I have youth in my side and hope in my heart that things will
improve not just for myself, we do not want your pity
But I would ask that next time you pass by someone in a
sleeping bag yes maybe a little unkempt take a moment to ask
why
Did we choose this existence that has become our way of life,
perhaps you could just acknowledge us as you pass by
We all had different lives once, circumstances, debts, loss of
a loved one, mental health issues reduced us to live this way

If tomorrow you just noticed one of us, paid it forward with a kind word, hot drink just maybe you will have helped change someone's day.

Three Little Words

Three so very little words yet such a lot they say
How I wish I had the right to say them to you today
Three so very little words yet they never can be said
By me, to you not ever only maybe in my head
Three so very little words yet now nothing is the same
Everything is more serious not quite so much a game
Three so very little words that I should not feel for you
But no matter what I tell myself the fact remains I do
Three so very little words that say simply I love you
And ideally the next line is that you should love me too
Three so very little words but it is just not meant to be
There is no happy ending here not for you and not for me
Three so very little words that came too late for us
One word will do and it's goodbye, a clean end without much
fuss.

When tomorrow dawns, it will be exactly a week since we last spoke and I am leaving you some flowers at your door
As I leave, I will gently knock knowing you cannot answer, how I wish I could see your smiling face just once more
You my friend of many years are so missed, I still expect to see you in the shop, I guess with time that will fade away
I hope you know how much loved you were, your caring heart and the friendship we shared will be with me forever and a day.

An Angel's Reply

When I read your poem, Alphabet of Cuddles, I found some of the words you penned
Were words from your heart that touched me so I am replying in poem form my friend
I'm not smart enough to use all the alphabet so I'm going to select two words for you
Hopefully the words I choose will resonate with how we often feel and bring comfort too
So, the first letter of the alphabet is A so Angel is the second word the first is Always
A Anyone can feel lost and overlooked at times I know that I indeed have such days
L Loneliness is a terrible companion felt by us all even when we are in a crowded room
W When we have lost a loved one, we have good days and dark days filled with gloom
A Another emotion is suddenly finding we don't know how to fill our time as life goes on
Y Yes family and friends are supportive which helps yet we yearn for the life that's gone
S So many memories in the early days but also someone's kindness makes you smile
A And you find yourself feeling okay, though dark days will come today life is worthwhile
N No matter who we are each of us have been comforted by a hug that is sincere

G Going about our busy lives I still try to smile and ask after people that I hold dear

E Everyone has a story so a kind word or listening ear can make someone's day better

L Let's pay caring forward it costs nothing let's do it often as there is an Alphabet of letters

----

Never let a day draw to a close without telling those that you care for just how much you love them so
Nothing in life is promised to us this was written in stone oh so many years ago
I try to live my life believing that if you give of yourself to others because you want to not because you should
Perhaps they will in time realise it is a priceless gift and learn to pay it forward, I know some who would
I realised that not everyone we meet in life shares my thinking and I cannot change that if it is not meant to be
I hope that most of us understand at one time or another that a random act of kindness is beautiful to see
Holding the door open for someone or smiling at the little old lady struggling up the street
We often in our busy lives rush past without noticing or taking just a minute to really look at people that we meet
If only they are two such little words but how often are they repeated by each of us every single day
Let's make them into two much more powerful words by being kinder to someone who comes our way
It is inevitable that we at some time in our lives wish for the impossible or a miracle or two
If we are honest, we even ask for things just for us, it is human nature that at times this we do
Just imagine though if during a part of today you went out of your way to do for another something just because you could

Then wait and see how you felt it is a wonderful feeling to do
a kindness to others when you both share something good
So just to humour me today take a moment and offer an act of
kindness to someone that you don't know
Then imagine that they in turn repeat the gesture because we
started a feeling so good that everyone nurtures it so it can
grow

My Vision

Before tomorrow's dawn I am going to wait for you again just in case, I hope I will find you here

I will lay flowers once it gets light in our childhood churchyard for on my last visit I felt you near

Not a single day has gone by in this first year without a thought, a tear or a need for you

Your vibrant personality in that tiny frame has left all who love you so very lost we know not what to do

I look for signs that you are near I talk to you each morning and you are my last thought every night

Are you here yet? Maybe if I go around to the far side of the church perhaps you are but out of sight

It is light now in my vision I have done the flowers for all those we love and miss, the hyacinths are for you

They bring to mind your beautiful smile and those kind all seeing eyes of just the brightest blue

I have to go now I have not felt you near or seen any signs to say that you were here with me

That is okay because you need to be closer to your home and put your arms around your family

We were not prepared for this day to come a year ago and yet, here we all are with our own memories of you

I hope you know that for many of us you have changed the way we think, for me at least this is true

Beyond the clouds in the sky and from the stars twinkling at night, know just how much you mean to us all

I still wish that we had you here but God had a plan for you
when he sent an angel on you to call
I think of our family as a beautiful building sadly over time
parts of it have crumbled away
I take comfort that it will be restored to its former glory when
we are all back together some day

There Is Nothing to Fear

I used to have a fear of death and dying,
I felt that that it came uninvited and in disguise
Until someone close whose life was ending
Showed me there was nothing to fear through his eyes
I watched as his dear face lost all of its pain
And tired eyes become suddenly alight
Though I wept as if my heart was breaking
I knew he felt safe to go to the place within his sight
I have found myself often when someone's life is nearly over
Wanting to whisper what's heaven like can you see inside?
Of course, I never found out the answer to this question
As my friend passed gently to the other side
I picture heaven as peaceful like a warm and cosy room
Or like a spring morning when all the flowers are in bloom
Or like a sunset on a hillside gently starting a new day
Or the tinkling of a fountain as the water shows us her display
No matter what Heaven is really like, we will all know by and
by
And when that time comes we cannot help but ask God why
That we cannot understand why he has packed our loved one's
case
Take comfort from the thought that they have moved onto a
very special place

Today I found an Angel calendar just the same as you every year my lovely sister got for me

It is a simple thing but it gladdened my heart and the November verse is something I hope you see

Life can sometimes be difficult we all have different burdens some harder than we can bear

But today I am filled with new strength and hope just because I know that I have an angel's care

Happy Christmas to everyone those gone, those still here the New year brings us hopes and dreams however big or small

Look for signs for your angel hears what's in your heart and listens to them all

----

Please Wait for Me

I am ready Mum if the time must be now
I think in my heart that I knew it somehow
But though I am ready will you still wait for me
To make the journey home, your face to see
Once more I want to hold onto your hand
To look into your eyes to show you that I understand
I want to hold you close as we say our goodbye
And to tell you how I love you and will till I die
I love you so much and although my heart is so sad
I know you are tired with the struggles you have had
Please wait for me Mum there are things I must say
I need to share your life for just one more day
Please wait for me Mum though you are surrounded with love
The family are all with you and Dad is waiting above
So selfless your love for me and it has always been so
Yet I am being selfish in not wanting yet to let go
Not really selfish for I know that it is time we must part
But I want to tell you just once more of the love in my heart
Please wait for me Mum before you journey to a far better
place

Please God hear my prayer and let me just once more know
my mother's embrace

My Prayer

I said a prayer for you today and I am certain that God heard
For I felt such peace within my heart although I heard no
spoken word
I said a prayer for you today just because I love you so
And sometimes in our busy lives I maybe forget to let you
know
I said a prayer for you today that you may find some strength
within
To cope with all the memories that inevitably this day will
bring
I said a prayer for you today that the loss that is with you every
day
Is touched with some inner pride at how hard you fought for
her to stay
I said a prayer for you today that love will help to heal your
heart
And hope you know that she is with you even though your
lives may dwell apart
I said a prayer for you today because I don't have the words
to explain
That as a Mother I would have done anything to protect you
from this pain
I said a prayer for you today that on the days when your loss
is hard to bear
If you close your eyes and listen to your heart you will know
that she is with you everywhere

I said a prayer for you today and I just wanted to take this opportunity to say
Please take comfort in the knowledge, everyone who loves you is thinking of you on this Memorial Day

----

When tomorrow dawns, it will be exactly a week since we last
spoke and I am leaving you some flowers at your door
As I leave, I will gently knock knowing you cannot answer,
how I wish I could see your smiling face just once more
You my friend of many years are so missed, I still expect to
see you in the shop, I guess with time that will fade away
I hope you know how much loved you were, your caring heart
and the friendship we shared will be with me forever and a
day

Never get tired of being that special friend with time to offer
a listening ear or a good heart
We give of ourselves to others because we can that's when
from within our kind nature does start
You, I and many other folks during our lifetimes will sadly
have been hurt by someone we hold dear
Yes, we cry and question why this is so but in time the path
we tread once again will become clear
During these difficult stages of course, we question those who
hurt us and I believe we doubt ourselves too
Yet when the road ahead is less bumpy, we look back, learn
and yes, we stay the same because it is all we know how to do

----

The Photograph

Looking at the photographs of yesterday, I found that a tear ran down my cheek

Not because it was a sad occasion, quite the opposite so much love I couldn't speak

So many generations of the family gathered together also friends and acquaintances only that day met and made

Yet it was another priceless memory to add to all the others in the foundations of the footpath on which my life is laid

In the flashing of a camera or as in today the selfies and snapshots we seem to take with our phones just because we can

We get the opportunity to relive these special moments which are too rare and therefore priceless to every woman or man

After each of these events I say to myself that we must not let so much time pass before we come together as a family

Yet life gets in the way again and again so until next time yesterday was more than enough and meant the world to me

----

Yesterday morning the fridge magnet, I had of yours woke me as it fell as I picked it up I
heard you say "please don't be afraid"
So real my dream of the night before I felt you next to me as you said I'm always here as you walk the foundations already laid
I lay there in the darkness and realised that my pillow was wet from tears I didn't know that I had cried
I remembered that you chastised me for not realising that even when I felt alone you were always by my side
So, I want you to know that it comforts me that you seem to appear when for a moment I temporarily lose my way
I do question why this happens because I am so blessed for which I always give thanks every single day
You know how I cope the best when I can keep everything under control but this cannot always be
It's a fault of mine that you used to nag me about where I would not ask for help but it's so alien to me
Anyway, I'm alright and I took such comfort that as in life before you left you still give a guiding hand
With love in abundance in the family I am so proud to be a part of there is nothing lost without something gained I will learn from this so I can understand
When the road ahead seems too long and each new step so hard to take
Put your trust in me and with your hand in mine this new journey together we can make

It's inevitable at times in all our lives that we will falter and feel too weary to carry on

It is at these times we must rely on those who care to take your weakness and make you strong

Every day I count my blessings for all that has been gifted to me to share

Remember that for others when life gets tough, they may not have anyone to care

Life's journey is not promised to be more ups than downs many times we each may fall

I try to take what I learn from each experience and pay it forward to one and all

----

A Special Friendship

Each and every one of us has a story some which we get to witness by chance, some we are never meant to know

I hope I stay receptive to others pain because it helps me to not only right my world but to care more and to grow

We are very different I talk incessantly, you're more a straight talker that makes me catch my breath at times at the black and white

But your logic as I know how much you care actually does stop my world revolving and restores it to be alright

We have had many conversations and I hope that we have taught each other things that before we maybe did not see

I have tried to live my life believing that through its ups and downs though challenging at times they are shaping me to who I aim to be

I would be lying if during my journey where tears were more prevalent than smiles, I have not asked why is this happening to me

Where at times you said to me you appear condescending, I hope now that you realise that was never true at all

We are each individual for a reason some of our weakness is another's strength that is there to catch us when we fall

I hope you see yourself as I see you with a heart full of kindness and whose friendship, I have been blessed to receive

Regardless of the journey we still have left to travel, the path on which we met or even why is priceless I believe

----

Mother's Day

Today on this Mother's Day in heaven there are two special mums sitting side by side

I want to wish you joy together but my heart is full of so many tears that I have cried

Mum for many years now I have sent you my loving prayer on every Mother's Day

Not for a moment did I imagine I would be sending wishes to my sister too in this way

Her family here on earth are so lost they were not prepared; it was not her time to go

Tell God to ignite a host of candles and light the way so that she may know

That our love would build a stairway and if we could we would walk it for her today

So, we could hold her just one more time and say all the things we still have to say

Tell her I am wearing the angel necklace she gave me the last time we were together

Let her know that everywhere there are memories that will stay in my heart forever

Every one of us would give up everything for just a moment her face again to behold

We were not ready to say goodbye we were to live much more before this day did unfold

My prayer would be to send her home back to earth to be with her grieving family

I know through my pain it will not be granted it cannot and I know why and I see
So, wrap your arms around each other close your eyes and for just a moment, be still
Do you feel the love surrounding you Happy Mother's Day love you now and always will

----

As I could not delay it any longer, I have started painting the woodwork there are four doors on the upper floor.

I did one door last night and went down to make a cuppa and downstairs there are two more.

That's not to mention all the architrave, skirting boards and the spindles and banister rails on the stair.

Why am I telling you all this I hoped someone who loves painting may read this and hopefully care.

Seriously though painting white satin wood paint endlessly is so tedious I could possibly cry.

I have to get it done as the collie dog coming to stay next month will spoil it if it's not dry.

I have to keep changing from a biggish brush for me to a small one for all the fiddly bits.

It's all very nice having nicely plastered walls but the decorating side is getting on my nerves.

you expected a naughty word then didn't you as if

A Mother

When your child is little
And something makes him cry
Some magic cream, a hug from mum
How quickly those tears dry
When your child is bigger
And much too brave to cry
Mums still there to listen
She will try to reason why
When your child's an adult
And starting out with a new wife
Mum still loves you just as much
As when first she gave you life
But now life has gone full circle
Do you ever wonder why
Mum doesn't seem so happy
Or just who has made her cry
Do you take the time to wonder
Who could help to ease her pain
Does she wish her mum could cuddle her
And make life right again
We cannot always be responsible
For what happens to each other
But now maybe we will have some understanding
What it actually costs to be a mother

The Looking Glass

You are stood again before the mirror
As you have done many times before
There is no sticking plaster on your face
Nor is there an open wound that is sore
You are looking really closely now
Yet still there is nothing for you to see
It is because your illness is of the mind
And you question why this should be
You go back over events in your lifetime
Recall experiences both good and bad
You have survived some highs and some lows
So where has the control gone that you had
You look for why this is happening
Is it the type of job that you do
Can you only give so much of yourself
Before it takes too much of you
You question the things that have happened to you
Did you cope at the time or just bury them away
The years have passed by with knocks here and there
So has your past come back to haunt you today
It is your body's way of warning you
That for too long you have pushed yourself too far
You have coped, you have cared, you've laughed and cried
But you have forgotten just how important you are
You must face the doubts and the demons that haunt you
Bring them out and dissect them carefully one by one

And only when you discover that you love the person you are
Will you find that all of your demons have gone
This will be the hardest goal that you have set yourself
But I am confident that it is one you can win
Then when you stand once again before the mirror
You will know it is over and today your life can begin

There are no words for where to begin and what could anyone possibly say
To ease the pain and loss because of this tragedy that is in your hearts today
So, we have prayed and lit a host of candles to light up the stairway to heaven
How we all wish it was not your loved one leaving as she is too young at only seven
I did not know you as I'm sure nor did many who have left condolences for your family
Grief brings a community together and we hope in time this love for you will enable you to see
Your little girl will live on not just in your hearts but in the hearts of all those whose lives in which she played a part
She will be able to look down and say I made a difference with new safety measures and it will gladden her heart
Your own special star is now twinkling in the heavenly skies way up high on the wings of a dove
Take some comfort from all our prayers that your precious little one left this earth too soon but surrounded with love

----

Sisterly Love

Sometimes I cannot find the words of comfort to say to one that I love so dearly
To reassure you that in time I know that you will see your way more clearly
I would not promise you that next week next month or even next year that it will be okay
Yet this I will promise, that I will always be there for you every second of each new day
We seem to find it harder now that we are older, to put things back as they should be
We cannot pick ourselves up as yet, we have talked about this together you and me
So today I am sending you my love as I was reminded that it is priceless what we share
I know we need more time my beautiful sister but one day, together we will get there

----

Do you find yourself during this cold weather, like I do more and more every day

Wondering what a homeless man or woman's life was before they have to live this way

I feel as I put some money in their tin wanting to actually look into their eyes to see what they portray

To take time, slow my steps buy a hot drink and ask them who and how they are and listen to what they have to say

I remind myself daily when I complain about the weather or the frosted windscreen on my car

That the lady I gave my scarf to last week once upon a time had a good job and a flat above a bar

Or that man who followed me into the cafe hoping for a coffee to go was once a soldier who'd travelled far

Do you like me find yourself questioning why they are so vulnerable compared to where you are

Each homeless person will have a story to tell if we took time to listen what harm can that do

Maybe we will be surprised that only a couple of things going wrong for us and it could happen to me or you

So next time we walk by someone living in a way we may judge or even not really understand

Take just a moment to give him or her your gloves, money for a hot cup of soup for it costs nothing to offer a caring hand

I am for some reason much more aware now of the amount of people living on the streets up and down the land

Make a promise to yourself to do a kindness tomorrow to just one person just because you can let's make a stand

----

Love and Hate

Love and hate lie back to back, the hate word I can say is one I rarely if ever use

For such emotion to anyone is wasted as that person has nothing left to lose

The tongue such a powerful weapon I am amazed how some use it so well to inflict pain

I am so proud that you never retaliated to the tirade that had you in tears once again

Today you must heed my words and grow stronger and realise they are not worth the time of day

I know you are shocked beyond measure that anyone can even begin to behave in this way

I know your worth as do many you must feed on the love of those whose words ring out with truth and are sincere

You will continue on this journey not defeated, yes, a little broken but with the path in front quite clear

One day I promise it will be okay I cannot say when but just that it's waiting patiently around the bend

So, for me and this priceless love we share, promise me that no matter how badly this day began it will feel better before its end

----

Words are everything to me always have been whether spoken
or written down

Equally I try to listen to others words those said with a smile
or indeed a frown

For reasons that I don't want to go into I think at times I sadly
forgot to hear

Some questions with perhaps a deeper meaning from friends
and those I hold most dear

Anyway it has taught me that no matter how just lately the
days seem to be just rushing by

I like all of us at this time of year have shopping still to do
and cards and presents left to buy

That for some who have asked me stuff and seemed sad and
implied they may like my company

I needed to react better at the time as though I have reflected
afterwards this they cannot see

So I have made a tad early my New Year's resolution and
unlike quitting smoking this one I will not break

It is simply to listen to words spoken to me by everyone and
act upon them at the time this is one resolution I can genuinely
make

It is inevitable as this year draws to a close that we look back
at how the year has been
I personally have heard of new life beginning and the loss of
some now no longer seen
I have in my working life heard stories that for lots of reasons
I had not heard before
I have learnt from opening my heart to others that to be kind
is the way to be for sure
I have realised that though it is human nature to wish for life
to be easier at times for me
Somewhere a glimpse of untold sadness was meant to be
revealed so that I would see
How fortunate I am and my worries are trivial when today I
asked someone if they were okay
In my job I ask that frequently but every now and then the
recipient has a sad tale to portray
We all at times I believe become complacent and forget just
how very blessed is the life we lead
This year I have found myself humbled in the things I take for
granted when so many simple things others need
We all make New Year's resolutions quit smoking, get more
exercise we often fail but here's one we all can keep
Be kind to each other whether family, a friend or a stranger
remember them in your prayers each night before you sleep
Kindness is a priceless gift it costs you nothing in monetary
terms but to someone it feels like they just won the lottery

So, make that wish be nice just because you can pay it forward
wanting nothing in return it's wonderful try it and you will see

----

In my busy day serving customers conversation is usually, due to distance guidelines, hello and as they leave a take care
But in the quieter times sometimes a complete stranger or someone you know has a harrowing story to share
This week there have been lots of moments when I am just looking forward for my shift to end
Then you realise that the lady at the counter is not in a hurry to leave and you smile and let them know you are a friend
We all at times focus on the list of jobs we have still to do those last-minute presents still to buy
And yet I looked really looked at the lady and said are you okay and with that simple question she started to quietly cry
It matters not what she shared with me I knew of her recent sadness and she knew I cared and yet
The hectic pace day in day out of my working life and it was only when she loitered and between us eye contact was met
That I stopped short and after talking to her realised that these current restrictions on us all reach deeper than we see
Some people are lonely and lost every single day not just now and I who tries to care about others forget briefly how to be
Everyone has a story and some folk just now, strangers or even a neighbour is struggling daily in ways unless we ask we cannot know
I paused today and listened and afterwards it felt good to realise that a hand of friendship makes a difference that we all can offer and see it grow

Be kind always as one day it maybe you who needs a friendly
ear

I lit a candle in my heart the day you left us and it still burns for you today,

I cannot extinguish its flame until, you send me a sign from heaven to say

That the path you took away from us was well lit and you arrived where you are meant to be.

And that you are happy and surrounded by love Oh I would give up everything just to see.

I don't understand why it is so hard for I believe there is another life than this earthly one we once shared

Yet every day I bargain with God to let me just have a minute to let you know just how much we all cared

I pretend the wind is you whispering in my ear, the rain your tears mingled in with mine,

This last week every day I have read your poem over and over again I know every word on every line.

It's Christmas soon it will seem strange for us all, we will all have a moment I'm sure whilst we remember,

I will tell you again I love you so as I proudly put up my card from you that you sent me last December.

My lot laugh at me because I keep my cards for months after the occasion, recycle them Mum they say,

Oh, how pleased am I that I did not listen to them as every year you will still send me a card on Christmas day.

A Mother's love is unending it is with you each and every day.

She will always take time to listen to what you have to say

She may not always have the answer to what is causing you such pain

She will reassure you that eventually your world will be right again

Her love is like a warm cloak around your shoulders keeping you safe from harm

It reminds you if you are lonely, you just have to take her arm

A mother will always guide you but she will let you choose the way

She will tell you that even if you go wrong she walks with you each and every day

She knows that as you grow older others in your life will take her place

She will always hold you in her arms in only a mothers very special place

A mother knows when you're not happy and she quietly waits patiently to see

If you remember all she taught you that life is what you let it be

----

If only two such little words yet when we use them such powerful hopes dreams and regrets these words starting a sentence do convey

If only, we could have that yesterday back because now we realise that tomorrow was not promised, we had so much to say

If only and maybe I am sorry or I love you start a sentence that each and every one of us have uttered at some moment in every day

If only has taught me that of course I have regrets but "Only If" because I have indeed learnt from these, no more if onlys need walk my way

----

If we are as a family like bricks in a building and on each other we all can depend

I guess our parents did chisel and shape us to fit in some corner or end

Then us girls and our brother. all added extra rooms to the foundations and so gradually in time it grew

Then indeed our children developed the building further and I am so proud of it all old or new

How lucky are we as a family, that what was started so many, many years ago as our family chain

Is today this priceless creation that every year has value added to it again and again

In time some of the facade has crumbled away and some parts of it can no longer be seen

But for us and the future generations what a story of a families travel we all share for me it is the best journey on which I have ever been

----

Daddy's Bicycle

We have a bicycle that needs to start a new journey as our daddy does not need it anymore so sadly it must go

We have happy memories of our bike rides together so us his three boys came up with an idea that he would like and so

We wondered if anyone interested in it could place bids of how much they can afford and we could keep it open for a week or two

You see our daddy was looked after by Weston Hospice and they cared for him so nicely that we together decided this to do

Dad's bike is priceless to us boys because it reminds us all of the fun things we did as a family together

We will always have our memories but we know now that the hospice cares for someone's loved one every day, week and probably has forever

So, if we can raise some money for our dad's bicycle, we are going to donate it to the hospice as a thank you for looking after our dad

We hope if he is watching over us from heaven, he will be proud and pleased at our decision as that would help our hearts feel not so sad

----

The door to Heaven's home and garden never closes though it opens just one way,

This weekend I will ask an angel to make a delivery for me on this special day

The angel will bring you a parcel, I wish I could see your face as the ribbon is untied

I would give anything to hold your hand as you read all the words that are written just for you inside.

If the parcel arrives earlier than Monday my sister I know you, but promise me that you will wait,

Until your actual birthday before you open it so that together we who love you so can all celebrate.

For we all no matter what we are doing will as that morning dawns we will be still and think of you

Look up in heaven's garden ANG see the dove, on its wings it holds a message love you always and miss you forever too

----

Right that's it I must adjourn the boss has had a snooze to sort out his jetlag

I'm off outside whilst I have the chance to drink my coffee and have a fag

Then I must put on my studious head but I fear I left it in my new porch

I shall be typing quotes so bloody fast you will smell my fingers as they scorch

I actually type one fingered so that last bit was not really all that true

The warehouse stinks of solvents don't worry I know what I can do

I will tell him it's me that pongs as I have no perfume left not any not at all

If he hasn't bought me back a gift Boots the chemist in his lunchtime he can call

Now I really must sign off for now for I still haven't polished the office cat

He just rang to say the traffic's bad oh three bloody cheers for that

----

I listened to the song that my son sent me in my lunch hour today entitled You'll never walk alone

The words inevitably make you go to a place in your memories where you felt sad and on your own

I believe as we get older we each will try and glimpse the future and wonder what lies ahead

Something you read in the news or the illness of a friend or family member fills your heart with dread

Words in a song filter into our sub conscience sometimes the lyrics make us happy other times we feel sad

A tune from long ago on the radio in your car reminds you of a time or a place that you once had

Yet it is up to us to choose how to be, live your life well, be giving share with others and above all please be kind

For the person who you saw last today may have been uplifted by your hello or smile you may just find

We are all so very busy with our lives and I am blessed so far with the life I was given to live

Today I was reminded again with the words in the song that I am not alone and I still have so much more to give

----

These last few weeks I have struggled to walk the path with some who take more than they seem to give.

Oh I know it is not for me to decide how others behave when everywhere in this moment someone is just trying to live.

I have learnt more valuable lessons during this time that I hope I can pay forward to others along the way

It saddens me that for some everything is black or white or just right or wrong or night will always follow day

I know in time when this sadness passes I will resume the path with those who do not see life's experiences as I am blessed to do

Knowing that the heaviness in my heart and the tears I cry were necessary and are all part of the friendship I shared with you

if we could we would talk like we used to about the different people who crossed our path and why we knew them but we never questioned why we two met

I guess we may never find the answers my friend but it matters not for your friendship needs no explanation and it's one I will never forget

----

Each of us can be likened to a jigsaw we are unique and come in all shapes, colours and sizes
And just like the picture the puzzle reveals we have an image but also we have disguises
To the onlooker we have our everyday face but like the unfinished jigsaw some pieces of us are harder to find
So, on the days when we seem to be not who you know take a moment to wonder if we have a lot on our mind
For those of us who struggle and we all do at times remember that we are trying to make all our pieces fit into place
So, help us to find that elusive edge piece as your time and effort may put a happy image back on our face

----

I have just been to post some letters with my second youngest grandson he is two

We posted invoices to Basingstoke and Cambridge and one to Timbuktu

The last address was obviously fictitious I just wrote it because it kept in rhyme

My grandson's little legs compared to my long strides meant we walked quite out of time.

I realised how old I am getting as before we were even half way there

My mind was scrambled with his questions about what's that, whose that and where

I thought I was a modern nanny I know the words to the wheels on the bus

I have bathed them all and changed their nappies I never make a fuss

But this constant chattering well I can't remember mine talking so much when they were small

I know you are probably thinking I'm getting crabby well I don't think I am at all

Seriously I admire his elocution levels after all he probably gets that from me

Imagine if he talks like this at two I will never cope when he turns three

If I had a pound for each time he has said nanny or asked me what was that

I would be on a Caribbean island by teatime under a parasol
sipping cocktails in my best sun hat
I suppose although I love all my grandchildren more than
words can say
I do not remember signing up to work with him and his dad
all day

Sometimes just for a moment when a new day starts, I forget
then a reminder makes me realise at times I actually don't
know who to be

Those of you who know me well will understand that I think
of ten jobs at once that need doing and I am hard to live with,
please don't think I'm feeling sorry for me

I say often in my poems that everything we experience good
things bad things there is something to be learned and we will
indeed see it when the time is so

Today I have learned that although at times like today when I
get it so very wrong, I can learn to take small steps and in time
who I am well I will always know

I just now went to close my back door on the thunder and to stop the rain from coming in,

When down the garden on my arbour seat that's sheltered by the clematis a robin sat within,

I stood quietly watching it walk back and forth across the slatted seat.

At each end before it turned to go back the other way it looked at me which made my heart feel sweet,

And then it hopped onto the garden fence and gradually made its way closer to me

Even before he started to sing, I shed a tear for I knew just what in him I was to see

There are always signs from our loved ones in heaven but today this one sent from those above

Seemed to literally be heaven sent to me at just the right time to remind me of their love

That little bird for ten minutes or more sat on the fence chirping out his song

I hope he knows what joy his presence gave to me to last me all this day long xx

----

Do you ever feel so melancholy that though you have been up for hours you didn't see the blueness of the sky

Or in the place you have gone to, too be alone, in the trees above you, you didn't notice the flock of birds flying high

Even though your sadness is not for you well a small part is, it is for others for whom you love and care

Have you as the hours pass by whilst you reflect suddenly felt that you are not alone that someone unseen is there

I admit my place to be today is somewhere where so many lost loved ones rest, belonging to many at peace side by side

Each and every one of us has visited such a place because we believe somehow only they see the tears that we have cried

It's getting dark now and I need to go home so those who love me do not worry about how I am or where I may be

Though the emotions I feel today have not been resolved when tomorrow comes I will feel more at ease and that comforts me

Today is not the first time nor I'm sure will it be the last that I find myself in this spot but each time I'm blessed that every time I'm here I feel

When my thoughts have overwhelmed me it is like though I'm still alone someone's arms are hugging me and I believe it's real. A guardian angel watching over us.

So, this property hunting well to be honest it's quite an ordeal
Let me tell you of some the abodes we have been to view
There was the basement flat with how many bloody stairs
Then the bijou place where you could cook tea whilst sitting
on the loo.
Then there was the seafront apartment with a couple of cats
sat around the sink
The shared landing and stairway needed more than a lick of
paint I think
At one to see the rare outside space I walked through spiders'
webs and hit my head on a lamp
Whilst he admitted it was slightly elevated SLIGHTLY, I
could have my own skateboarding ramp
Oh, so many different residences have we now seen and to be
honest I could knit a decent one quicker
And then tonight we are going to view a place for the second
time where we if we like it get our very own clicker.
Yes, now I have got your attention haven't I you are curious
as to exactly just in what and where we may soon dwell
So, I will try to keep you updated as after today no more
looking until my poor swollen feet get well

If I could cook which most of you know I can't today I would bake a cake

On the sixty-five lit candles some special wishes I would make

Wish one would be that those I cherish never tire of hearing what they mean to me

My second wish would be that one day the next generation world peace they will see

I would wish next that we all take today to remember those who are in despair

Wish four would be that just for a moment someone shows them that we do care

Next I would wish that we all believe that happiness is not just for others

It is there if we search for it for son's daughters' fathers and mothers

My last wish is that just for a moment you would close your eyes my friend

And when you open your heart such joy is yours for taking just around the bend

---

I knew today was going to be different as soon as I rose from my bed

A bit like Worzel Gummidge I had got dressed wearing the wrong head

As I walked outside what to you would be leaves rustling in the breeze

To me it was as if the wind had whispered will you listen to me please

I paused for a few minutes to see if there was more for me to hear

I knew someone I loved was with me for not for a moment did I fear

It does not matter what my message was as I cannot truthfully be sure

My mind was playing tricks and was just reading what was in my heart before

I guess we all have times when we feel life is not as it should be

I advocate that life is what we make it so what is it that bothers me

We are all made different for a reason no one always right or always wrong

Every day will not be perfect but we should always try to get along

I believe for every cloudy day eventually the sun is going to shine

So, I have put on my normal head so once more me I can
define
I am glad for whatever reason I had to learn a new lesson in
life today
Why worry about what we cannot change today is tomorrows
yesterday

Isn't it strange how when you are emotional or overtired because you couldn't sleep as your thoughts kept you awake

That watching the rain run down your windowpane is to you something more because your mind-set gives it a different take

Today the raindrops to me represented tears from heaven not just for me but for all those whose hearts are heavy today

It comforts me to think our loved ones in heaven cry with us they hear our prayers they want the rain to wash the pain away

I stood outside work and suddenly the wind intensified I watched as the branches of the fig tree swayed and suddenly as if by an unseen hand

The wind eased but above my head four or five leaves drifted away and I imagined they settled out of sight in a peaceful land

----

Heaven Sent

Thank you for all my birthday wishes from my lovely family
I thought as I have turned fourteen, I would write a poem from me
To my mummy look for me in the rainbows when I am on your mind
I am the treasure at the other end that one day you will find
When you sing which you often do I'm there singing the words with you
I often sing here in heaven's garden I must get my love of music from you
My eldest brother Brad you love your music but we definitely like different bands
If we could have gone to a concert together we would have to stay in separate stands
George, I watch you when you do your boxing well actually I mostly close my eyes
You are really good and have grown so tall which comes as a bit of a surprise
For though I look like Mummy my stature is like Charlie I guess I'm petite in size
Charlie and I share the love of creating things but he has more patience than me
My twin sisters I love watching you have your hair done you are growing up so fast
Your still young so you can see me when I visit and I know that this sadly will not last

Nanny has a memory box in her hallway I can see what precious things she has inside
The feathers, pennies, the robin in the garden are from loved ones who here in heaven reside
I see all of you when you visit my resting place and the beautiful flowers you leave for me
I so wish you could turn or feel me sitting on the churchyard wall for I am there you see
I love my earthly family, and the love you share is special and reaches way up to me here
So, on this my birthday please know that though out of sight your love for me keeps me near

----

Give Up a Coat This Christmas

Got a new coat for the winter
I did once again this year
Valued my old one for some reason a little differently
Edie a homeless lady it suited her she was such a dear
Upon her face appeared the most beautiful smile
Please she said can we talk for just a short while
And what I learned about this gentle lady that day
Can never be repeated simply because what she had to say
Opened my eyes and taught me that we must not judge another
Anyone of us could be her, a sister, neighbour, friend or mother
This Christmas my old coat is the most priceless gift I think I ever gave
Thank you, Edie, for sharing your story, may you always stay so proud, so brave
Homeless people are just the same as us, a twist of fate and it could be you or me
I feel privileged that you though so very cold shared your life so that I may see
Somehow, I know I will never forget your words or at times recall your all-seeing face
CHRISTMAS is for giving and my best gift this year will be without a doubt your warm embrace

----

The Reflection

On the other side of the mirror there for some is a reflection we cannot see
To the image in this side of the looking glass we question why this should be
Hopefully the person looking back at us is more prevalent, this means we are having a good day
At other times when we feel a little lost, we ask the us how long are they going to stay
To the person that we can all see because this image is the one life has chosen us to share
We ask that though you may not understand, for our hidden self, love us both enough for it helps us to know you care
I have been that person reflected in the glass who was not familiar but it was me
So be kind to everyone try not to judge us, what we feel is real but invisible to see

----

An Angel Waits

I know now that an angel is winging her way to earth, when she arrives, she will watch over you and wait patiently by your side

She will walk unseen between your loved ones as they spend priceless moments with you, she sees the tears we all have cried

Her gentle hand on their shoulders will feel like a butterfly's wings as she offers comfort for them to face what lies ahead

When they leave to go home and rest before tomorrow dawns, she will stay with you to prepare and comfort you instead

Your angel already knows just how beautiful and tranquil it is beyond the skies and what awaits through heaven's door

When the time to leave is nearly upon you I believe that you too will see it and be at peace and not afraid anymore

I will forever cherish those precious hours tonight with you and I will keep your goodbye and hug nestled in my heart

If our goodbye was indeed the last we get to share, safe journey my friend and God bless you but he did that from the very start

----

Meant to Be

They say our life is already planned
And today I found this to be oh so true
I have always wondered where my poetry would lead
I know now that it was my path to you
When I penned that family tree poem to you
I was a little afraid that it might offend
It was the first poem I had written since my mum died
Yet it was easy, like writing to a special friend
I have always believed that everyone has a soul mate
Today that is how you described me
I feel as if a part of my heart has been unlocked
I'm glad that it was you who held the key
My first instinct today was to give you a call
From the start the evening didn't go as I planned
Yet I realised that it did not matter at all
For fate had already played its first hand
I feel sad for all the years that we've wasted
Though like you said the past is best left in the past
I just feel blessed that the future is all ours
In my heart I know our relationship is to last
I long for the day that I can meet up with you
Exchange stories of the lives we have had
To see if this incredible feeling of oneness
Is something we share because of our dad
Regardless of where our lives take us
For I believe what will be, will be so

I'm so glad that you feel I'm your soul mate
My feelings are the same, I just wanted to let you know

My Tapestry of Memories

Since you left us, I have been creating a garden tapestry of
memories

Which I hope to finally complete by this year's eleventh of
November

It will be the second birthday we can only share with you in
our hearts

So, this patchwork of colour will help me recall your beauty
and to quietly remember

In each corner I have planted for you, and the date clusters of
beautiful red poppies

On the next row an abundance of daffodils they are standing
so proud and so tall

Next in line is a sea of the most remarkably delicate bluebells

They remind me so much of your eyes this row is my most
favourite of all

Underneath these I have chosen to plant just randomly some
snowdrops

These represent the tears that so freely for you still, do I shed

If I look out of my window and look at the creation that I have
made

I imagine that you are sleeping and at peace in this colourful
bed

At the bottom I have planted three rows of different coloured
roses

People associate roses more than any other flower to represent
their love

For me they are the quilt that I have gently placed over your shoulders
In one part of my tapestry nothing seems to grow it seems to be shaded from up above
I believe for the time being that corner will stay empty for it echoes a space in my heart
I take comfort that one day it will fill with colour when we are reunited and never again will dwell apart

----

White Feathers Lead to Me

I dreamt last night that there was a staircase of white feathers
that I should try to find
In order for this to happen first I must sit quietly and bring
thoughts of you to my mind
I closed my eyes and I even held my breath after a while I felt
something touch my hair
On opening them there before me was my walkway and a
white feather on the bottom stair
As I walked up each stair slowly candles flickered and lit up
above my head quite high
I don't know if I was alone, it didn't feel so but I couldn't see
you and this made me cry
The staircase seemed endless at times and white feathers
fluttered down and settled like a carpet on the ground
I felt certain that I heard footsteps but there were just the
shadows made by the candlelight when I looked around
I paused as suddenly I knew I was no longer alone as I felt a
presence at first I did not understand
In that moment I realised that though I could not see you, you
were beside me and had taken hold of my hand
I was crying properly now for once more I could see you
clearly and I tried to memorise your beautiful face
When it was like someone had draped a blanket around my
shoulders I felt myself wrapped in your warm embrace
I opened my eyes as aloud I said Oh I love and miss you each
and every minute of any given day

From up above millions of white feathers floated down and I know what you were trying to say

The candles flickered and it was harder to see and I felt that these special moments were coming to an end

It mattered not for I now know how to bring you to my mind I just climb the staircase and find you waiting just around the bend

----

Thank You

I have a written a poem to say thank you
For helping me to grow
I have learnt lots of different things
That before nursery I did not know
One of my favourite things is dressing up
But I love milk and biscuits time I do
I think sometimes I was really well behaved
Because instead of one biscuit I got two
There are lots of different Aunties
Key worker Auntie Tina mainly looks after me
She sometimes asks me for a kiss and a cuddle
But I don't do that now but I did when I was three
My best friend at nursery of all the girls is Amber
I hope she likes me the most out of all the boys
I really enjoyed last year when we did the Trike-A-Thon
We raised money to buy new books and toys
I do not want to go to big school yet
My Mummy and Auntie Tina say it will be okay
Apparently I just need to have confidence
I will find it at nursery if you let me stay
Auntie Karen is in charge of everyone
Angie taught me to write my name
Auntie Tina knows everything that I like to do
Matching dinosaurs is a really fun game
Lots of new children take our places next term
I hope sometimes you will remember me

I promise to be brave in September Auntie Tina
So, you can be proud of who you helped me to be

A Mum's Garden

A Mother plants a special garden from the moment her child
is born
It isn't filled with plants and flowers or has an immaculate
green lawn
Yet she nourishes it with loving care and sits back to watch
you grow
She tends to it every day and with more love than you can
ever know
She keeps you safe from hidden dangers and guides you along
the way
Each new achievement that you make gladdens her heart
every day
She is there to catch you when you stumble her helping hand
is always near
She knows one day you will take another's hand she prays
they too will love you dear
She may not when you are fully grown always be there to stop
you from feeling afraid
She just hopes that you take comfort and strength from the
garden path that she laid
She and you are much older now and she reflects on the
garden laid with love from her guiding hand
She gets so much joy from her creation and now that you are
a mother too, you finally understand

If we imagine ourselves many years ago, as a seed carried by the wind or perhaps dropped by a bird in flight

Over time we take root and grow to be who we are today, liken yourself to a tree if you might

Some of us will grow tall and strong, it's branches thick and sturdy, and secure where it may stand

Others grow less uniformly; branches break off and become weaker and reshoot in less fertile land

Yet each and every tree will tell a story, some are straightforward, as clear as night inevitably will follow day

Others their narrative is more complex, life twists the smaller branches so it's uncertain what they have to say

Yet whether humans or trees, each is different for a reason, it was destined to be this way long, long ago

I wonder if when our leaves fall to the ground, we each actually learn just what we were meant to know

----

Learning from the Young Ones

Not long ago we lost a loved one and my grandsons Mummy
went outside to cry

His Daddy explained to him that if your heart is broken too
much sadly you will die

I taught his Mummy that you should always tell the truth and
leave no word unspoken

Unfortunately, now if he sees us cry he asks fearfully if it
means our hearts are broken

We think we know what they understand how they interpret
what they see and hear

Yesterday he taught me something that filled my supposed
knowing heart with cheer

It matters not what he said to me only that I listened to what
he so wanted me to know

It was priceless and so innocent but a moment to store in my
heart and never let it go

This little person whom I'm blessed to spend time with on
Nanny sleepover days

Has no idea how his comment as we did a jigsaw puzzle
together put my pieces back together in the simplest of ways

Speak Carefully

The tongue has no bones in it but if is used carelessly can be strong enough to break a person's heart
Always be careful with your words for once spoken they are sometimes hard to take back once you start
If you are repeating the same words over, one of you has stopped listening or perhaps has ceased to care
So, speak clearly so as not to be misunderstood, it may help or maybe it's time sadly with regret to end the times you share
Take time to reflect and look back on the path we have taken, decide if we should journey onwards on the road, we tread
Or evaluate everything we value most in our lives and begin a completely new adventure with those we love instead
Whatever choices we make I always hope that everyone has another to accompany them and leave a second set of footprints in the sand
For loneliness is a terrible companion, instead imagine we all have just one special someone who walks beside us holding tightly onto our hand

----

We Remember

I sold five poppies whilst at work and saw many more on the
collars of those on their way to remember today
I would have loved to join my voice to the throngs at services
everywhere, but I bowed my head to pray
Up and down the country people of every age came together
and took the time to recall
Those who lost their lives fighting for a better world for you,
for me and for one and all
I like to imagine heaven resounding with the united singing in
services across the land
I smiled at a young boy walking proudly to our church with
his parents, too young to understand
I prayed for the fallen and those left behind and for all those
who are lost and on their own
I prayed that someone will hear their plight and comfort their
neighbour so they need not be alone
For on this day, we will not forget and we will remember with
pride and with love
After all it is as it was written long, long ago and taught to us
all by the lord above
So today for every poppy worn by each of us, every prayer
and every tear that fell
Love was there in everyone, remembering, caring, sharing
and together we did them proud as well

The New Trolley

The news at ten has finished the bubbly weather forecaster
tells us the south is due lots of snow
Marvellous I am thinking for the white stuff when delivering
newspapers is not much fun as I know
Trust me the Daily Mail when sodden does not make for a
good morning breakfast read
The red ink used on The Sun tabloid well when it gets wet my
how that stuff can bleed
The TV and Radio Times magazines, yes, the snow does run
off their glossy front cover
The inside pages a different matter you have no idea if it's
BBC Eggheads on now or Celebrity Big Brother
Anyway the snow has now gone past the top of my wellies
and has reached my arthritic knees
I don't think the pages on that People's Friend will dry out oh
bring the sun out please
Another thing whoever designed the delivery bags and
trolleys for this job, I bet it was a man!
Which did kind of get me to thinking I may have to come up
with a money-making sure-fire plan
You see the delivery conveyances do not keep the papers dry
and as for coping with the uneven roads
Yesterday when I got home after my round I discovered I had
given a lift to a couple of slimy toads
Also they do not take into account that people are all sorts of
different sizes and stature

The wheels on mine squeaked and groaned as I pulled it along,
I bet it is as old as Margaret Thatcher
Anyway I digress as I think I may have come up with what I
think could be a very sound idea
The postmaster will shake his head and tell you that I only
usually have just one of these each year
Seriously I am going to design a waterproof, windproof, non-
squeaking wheels all singing and dancing Trollette
It will be designed mainly with women in mind as we seem to
be the most reliable in this job as yet
I think the material I choose will have to be suitable so as to
be clearly seen when it's dark
I need it to be weighted at the bottom but not too heavy as
though I am good I'm no longer a spring lark
Anyway I must away as I have things to do designs to draw
and tweak what will be the finishing touch
If you have any helpful suggestions leave me a note in your
letter box I look forward to hearing from you very much

Getting Old

I am old and I am frail and I recently fell
So, I have been in hospital you see
Now I am back home, I live on my own
How can I possibly take care of me
My body it seems has suddenly grown weak
Yet my mind well that still is okay
I can tell you the name of our Prime Minister
And I know what the date is today
My eyesight is rapidly fading
I have cataracts in both eyes you see
I admit that I sometimes don't notice
When I have spilt crumbs on my knee
I have lived alone for so many years now
I have always taken care of myself
Yet I feel a little discarded today
Like some long-forgotten book on a shelf
It seems like it was only yesterday
That I was cooking myself dinner or tea
Yet even though this sounds a bit silly
My bathroom seems so far away from me
I am old and I'm frail and my body is spent
I hope that each day I can get a lot stronger
For though I feel scared as to how I may cope
I do still want to live a while longer

90

If We All Could Give a Little Time

Dear God, I need desperately to win the lottery
Now before you get cross because I have asked for wealth
It is not for me personally to spend on frivolous things
You see I want to try and improve our National Health
Up and down every corner of our country lord
There are people lonely and, in such despair,
Every day the same or every visiting time
There is never a friend or family member there
Now with a bit of money God I was thinking
I could employ people who are blessed with a kind heart
So, they could make time to visit all these lonely souls
It is not much or enough but it would be a start
I could also employ lots of people to do their cleaning
The elderly are vulnerable so we could eradicate all these bugs
I would also ensure that all these lonely people
Were guaranteed at least some daily hugs
Now I appreciate that you are always very busy
But if you could just spare a moment or two
It makes me sad how some people get forgotten
I will await what I feel sure will be a positive response from
you

Reflection

I have come to a place that I often visit when I want to be alone to think, look back and reflect

The trees have shed their leaves creating a carpet over the churchyard leaving an air of neglect

My favourite tree is the Magnolia, it reminds me when it is in flower of an ornate chandelier

The blooms on its branches are like opaque bowls holding all the souls of those we hold so dear

The tree that I have come to see is old its branches are bowed and bent down yet its roots are strong

The first time I sat beside it was over forty years ago it makes me realise how time just marches on

As I look up at its height it takes me back to a time when I had lost my way eighteen years ago

It was Spring the tree was in full leaf I tried to carve a prayer in its sturdy trunk so that God would know

I only managed a few letters when I stopped for as I etched into the bark a globule of sap trickled down the letter K

I sat there thinking that the tree was crying with me but I will always believe that things changed from that day

The light is fading now the security light has come on at the house that lies behind the churchyard wall

The branches are casting shadows over the many resting places they remind me of arms outstretched to comfort all

Over the door that leads to the belfry where the bell ringers go a Magpie sits, just the one, that signifies sorrow

That is okay it's properly dark now and the wind has got up I
will look for the Magpies mate tomorrow
I am back again by my tree the wind and rain have whipped
up the fallen leaves it looks like the trunk has a blanket at its
base
A piece of fallen bark is lying on the wall sadly even this
strong tree the elements and nature over time will erase
If trees could talk imagine the stories they could tell of what
they have witnessed taking place around where they stand
I have at different times leant against my tree and felt I was
being hugged and comforted by an unseen hand
There are a few people in the churchyard now leaving flowers
and wreaths on their loved ones resting place
On the wooden archway a squirrel sits waiting its tail
twitching it is poised ready as off for nuts he prepares to chase
I shall leave in a little while somewhat saddened that for the
one who long ago suggested this learning quest for me
Will upon reading the words that I have penned will realise
that I am not yet receptive or perhaps yet ready to see
Yet I have learnt something else about myself that as yet I
cannot share with anyone but I take strength from all I learn
Just like this weathered tree I still have a way to go before my
journey ends no doubt with many a twist and turn
I hope when my friend reads these words even if disappointed
he will perhaps not yet but one day be able to see
That he has taught many things and I hope that he has perhaps
learnt just one small thought changing gift from me
For I have lived my life believing that in every experience
good or bad there is something from them that we must know
When we realise what was there to learn, pay it forward and
like this tree nurture it from its roots and see it grow

For the most precious gift we have to give is a gift that you give because you can, and never give expecting something in return

A simple but genuine act of kindness to another is priceless and to me it is the best lesson that long ago I was blessed to learn

----

Together Forever

We sat at the table eating breakfast you and I as we had done umpteen times before

Remember when you read the papers headlines whilst I scanned the back page for the rugby score

In this hazy world you live in do you recall any of the life we have shared together you and me

Over sixty years of wonderful memories, in July we will have been happily wed for sixty-three

The doctor on his visit yesterday said your body is healthy it is just your mind that's gone

He talked of places you could go to, I told him no here with me at home is right where you belong

Our son and daughter try to help they lead busy lives but they visit us on a Sunday every other week

The grandchildren still remember how you laughed when you discovered them as we all played hide and seek

Oh, how I long for the smell of your baking coming from the kitchen every Saturday between three and four

We would tidy up together and have a fruit scone with a cup of tea another thing that sadly is no more

You used to love the garden so I took you to the conservatory window to show you the crocuses in bloom

But you didn't see their beauty you were afraid and thought we were in some other person's room

As it was a sunny day, I thought a drive to the beach would be good you used to love to watch the tide

Nothing seemed familiar to you and you got quite agitated, once I had you safely home, I admit that day I cried

It is late now after a day exactly the same as yesterday and a tear runs down my cheek as I get up to switch off the TV

You rise from your chair and say what you always do, I forget your name but thank you for taking care of me

As you have always done last thing at night, it seems to soothe you somehow, you slowly brush out your hair

You see me behind you through the looking glass, and as usual you seem surprised to see me there

I pull the bed covers over you turn out the light and wait until your rhythmic breathing tells me you are asleep

Then because I know that you will not see me, I sit in our old bedroom chair and filled with despair I weep

Yet in the morning as another new day dawns, I will be there waiting and will be right with by your side

For to me who promised to love honour and cherish you this I will do so willingly my precious bride

----

The Mask of Life

How many people from all walks of life
Do you suppose hide themselves behind a mask
But we are all so busy going our own different ways
We rarely stop and take the time to ask
How many times have you been asked how you feel
Your reply is always the same I'm just fine
Why can't we be honest when things do go wrong
Because it takes courage to step over that line
We are all far too proud we don't admit we need help
We don't even share that we are feeling quite down
It is as if we are ashamed to say out loud we can't cope
So, we all don our masks like the clown
They say a trouble shared is a trouble halved
And it does help to talk out your fears
But you've done it, I've done it hidden the truth
Then wait until you are alone before you shed any tears
Is it a fault of ours that we carry our burdens alone
Are we all much too preoccupied to care
Or is it simply when someone needs a helping hand
Unfortunately, there isn't anybody there
How should we cope when we are worried or in pain
Or when we really feel deeply distressed
Alone? No, I know that I would want somebody there
To care, offer comfort or help me to see what is best
Wouldn't it be wonderful if just for one hour each day
We could all take the time to look and to see

That behind the mask there are tears in those eyes
And that one day it could be you or maybe me

Ode to Peter Dyson

The first ever time that I met you
We were introduced by my sister Sue
She had seen my corns and calluses
And had asked you to see what you could do
I was nervous and quite embarrassed
As I sat down in your special seat
But you kindly very quickly reassured me
That you had worked on all kinds of neglected feet
You donned a mask and selected an implement
Scraped, filed and scraped some more
After quite some time you took a breather
To show me the pile of debris on your surgery floor
Whilst you were quietly working a miracle
My sister sat with her newspaper solving a crossword clue
I think my incessant chattering, as I was anxious
Was getting on her nerves, between me and you
I am known for not thinking before I speak
Actually I'm renowned for this trait within my family
Personally I don't know why it bothers them
As that's just who I am, who I choose to be
Anyway I digress, by now I am feeling relaxed
My feet feel superb that in itself is really great
I said that your massaging them was better than sex
With that my sister was hurrying me out the gate
Seriously though I genuinely wanted to thank you
For although I know I will never have pretty feet

Your transformation made me feel that I could wear sandals
And even paint my toenails a bright shade of red, what a treat

----

One Day in Life's Journey

We each of us mainly hold the map that outlines our life's journey

Others at times will influence us on the path that we individuals have laid

When we look back we will see from our footprints where we have made mistakes

Hopefully these times we will learn from and wise decisions by us then are made

When the road we tread seems too difficult I try to think of others whose journey is sad

It is at these times I look ahead and I put myself back onto my chosen pathway

Because I had forgotten for a moment the blessed life so far that I have had

I remind myself next time my footsteps falter it is because there is a lesson I need to learn

That we know not of others we may pass on the long road that stretches before us

But maybe if we walk a while with them, together we may reach where the road ahead takes a right turn

For just a simple act of kindness, a smile or as you pass by to bid a perfect stranger hello

May be the nicest thing that happened to them on the day that by chance you met

So, on the next leg of your own journey let's pay it forward because we never can know

If one day we would wish for just someone to remember us
where others may forget

My Memory Tree

Today I have planted a tree of dreams in my garden it is invisible to others but not me

It has tiny white blooms on each branch inside each is a message that only I am meant to see

To read the words that are written I simply have to sit quietly and be still for a while

As the petals unfurls a loved ones written words warms my heart and makes me smile

Throughout the changing seasons my tree will continue to thrive and to grow

Though any visitors to my garden cannot see it, that matters not it is only for me to know

We can all of us plant a tree of hope or of memories of those we all miss so very much

I promise you that even if you are not a gardener it will flourish with loves tender touch

----

We your boys never expected or wanted to have to say
goodbye to you so soon

You are the best Dad we could wish for in the world we love
you up to the moon

Your illness has been up and down you had good times and
times when you felt bad

Some nights we dream it is all okay in the morning we
remember and we feel so sad

We wish we could go on one more camping trip cook
marshmallows on the barbecue

Promise to turn off our Xboxes and get to sleep like you so
often asked us both to do

We don't actually talk about what's in our hearts but we see
you are tired every day

We want to know if you are as scared as us but again this is
another thing we don't say

Nan said that when people leave us they are at peace and see
something we can't see

She said you will be free of pain and will always be watching
over my brother and me

We your boys are not ready to say goodbye Dad remember
when you fixed my bike

We still have so much stuff we want to share before you find
out what heaven's like

We know even though we don't say it that on our birthdays in
October and November

You may not be here to celebrate with us I wish we could have a card to remember

Boys don't keep cards and stuff but this year a card would be the best present we had

Every night we can look at our card and say not goodbye but goodnight and love you Dad

We cannot yet understand what it will be like to not get a funny emoji or our phones pinging with a text

We pray that every day your still here we get brave enough to cry with you or deal with what happens next

So many things we want to say but talking about it makes it real and we don't want it to be true

We just hope you know that when you have to leave, a piece of our hearts will break away so you take our love with you

----

I'm stuck in a line of slow-moving traffic to my left I watch
the old lady put down her shopping bag as she opens her paint
peeled front door
The car in front of me is moving forward we are off the old
lady is not in my line of vision anymore
What life has she behind that neglected door, is anyone able
to tidy it up a lick of paint would brighten it up no end
Is she lonely does anybody visit her from one week to another
either a family member or perhaps a lovely friend?
Up the hill the lights turn red and without really looking
across the road between the cars runs a tiny little boy
He looks too young to be out on his own keep him safe as he
runs his errand lord for he must be someone's pride and joy
I must seem miserable with these words I write but actually
I'm not for I'm very lucky truly blessed indeed with my lot
I just wondered whilst the traffic is slow and I see all these
different people going about their day and yet I know not what
Each hour each day if all the people that I notice as I travel
this same stretch of road almost every week
Are they all happy with someone who cares about them who
stops to lend a hand where needed if indeed any help they seek
So, I thought that today instead of taking for granted that
happiness is a given thing and mine alone today to hold
I think I am going to appreciate every little thing I see and
hear and hope that my joy accelerates to others along life's
busy road.

When or should I say if this pandemic crisis comes to an end
for I guess we cannot really as yet be sure
Will we all go back about our daily lives in exactly the same
way as we each lived them before
Those who have lost loved ones to Covid19 or the NHS staff
who have seen suffering that we cannot comprehend
Not forgetting those who in isolation who had no family to
check on them it could be us without a friend
Have we learnt anything about ourselves in these difficult
times or perhaps helped just one stranger by offering a helping
hand
Or outside of the virus statistics remembered that somewhere
a child is being abused and they don't understand
All the statistics of cancer deaths child abuse and violent
partners are still happening but now not today's headline news
The press hound the government watch their every move and
criticise but do they know better let's hear their views
These past few weeks as I'm still working I have heard about
customers hopes and fears yet before I probably couldn't
recall their name
Behind every door there is a story and I'm blessed to have
shared chapters with a few yet still I felt some shame
We are all so busy with our lives and yes, we all try to take
time to listen or help someone who one day could be you or
me

So, God willing when life returns to what we see as normal I hope that if I have learnt anything from this frightening time it is be kind for it's wonderful to see

----

We all at times I believe even though we are blessed and lucky in what we are fortunate to share

Have that impossible dream, hope or wish for something that is life changing to help those for whom we so care

I always get the most pleasure from giving of myself just because I can an act of kindness that makes someone smile

A simple thing it can be, maybe doing a kind turn for an elderly neighbour who has been unwell for a while

Or saying "how are you today" to a stranger in a queue and because you asked it actually brightened their day

We are all so busy going about our lives that at times we don't notice that others are struggling and have lost their way

I have for some reason today, perhaps an item in the news or a heart-warming programme shown on the TV

Found myself thinking of people I know that I don't see as often as I should I question why I have let this be

But sadly though I have written a letter or message to catch up on my news and theirs too

I know a few weeks or months from now I will be thinking that I have let time pass again since I made time for you

I guess the message in this missive is when life for us all is so busy and the days just fly so swiftly by

Something or someone makes us remember to not wish for the impossible but enjoy what's close at hand I am going to try

----

Miss You So Much

The rain has eased a little, the wind has dropped and the early morning air seemed quite still

There you stood as if you were waiting at the top of what ever since I have called your hill

I walked past you to where I knew I was going and delivered the newspaper through the door

As I returned the security light went out from behind me and sadly, I could not see you anymore

Every door I went to, every path that I pulled the paper trolley down with its noisy uneven wheels

I knew you walked behind me I felt your presence nearby, at times you were close upon my heels

As I approached number 37 you clearly said I remember this climb be careful where you place your feet

So, I talked to you about lots of things as we continued together our journey down the street

The house lights were turning off and people I see each morning were appearing as they started about their day

I turned to see if you had seen that flock of birds but I realised I was alone, oh I still had so much more to say

My job was done I returned back home deep in thought and with a somewhat heavy heart

Until there in the quiet of the moment I realised what I should have known from the very start

I will cherish this morning's moments for it clarified that everything is exactly just as it should be

I hope you will understand just what a gift your guiding
presence this morning gave to me

There is a jar that sits proudly on the shelf by your chair in the home that together we shared

It is a comfort to me since you have gone and another reminder of how much for you that I cared

I know that though you're not physically here by my side you can be with me whenever I want you to be

Sometimes I think I see your reflection in the mirror so sure am I that I see you standing just behind me

At times I turn around and speak to you then I remember that you no longer in this home reside

I realise it is okay everything is as it should be some days are longer and my loneliness is harder to hide

I still say Good Morning to you as each new day dawns I imagine if I close my eyes and listen, I hear you reply

Last thing at night when another day ends it is always your name on my lips as a tear escapes from my eye

I know that you are still watching over me I take comfort in that as I go about my day my sweet love

We had such a happy life with lots of memories to cherish together between my home here and yours in Heaven above

----

Today I kissed your beautiful face for the very last time and I
held and stroked your hand
I talked to you words from my heart you would say ditto to
me if here I knew you would understand
I reiterated the promise I made last year to you and it is a
promise that I will never ever break
You taught me above all to give, you did it in abundance you
loved to give very seldom did you take
On Wednesday as so many of us come together to celebrate
you and your very love of life
Everyone of us will look out for that lovely man who
cherished every part of you, his precious wife
We will pray for your adored children that their hearts may
heal in the days and months to come
They never thought this day would come so soon when they
would lose their treasured Mum
The grandchildren who gave you such joy I could go on and
on with the names of those who cared for you
I don't believe you realised how many people's lives you
touched, it was quite simple it's what you do
As I left you today it still seemed surreal as if I was in a dream
and should not be happening at all
In the chapel a poem caught my eye in fact there were two
hanging in ornate frames upon the wall
One was called A Letter from Heaven and the words were so
comforting when death had torn our lives apart

It reminded me that all is well, you are at peace, we cannot
see you but you are not far for you will live on in our heart

----

Nine Balloons

Happy birthday to our darling granddaughter, today you will be nine

This year I have sent nine balloons to your home in heaven from mine

The white balloon is from Bradley because you went to sleep wrapped in his white baby shawl

He is old enough to remember, he wrote a message to you on his balloon that says it all

The purple one is from George it's his favourite shade he likes this colour the best

He sent you a little teddy bear you guessed it, he is dressed in a little purple vest

The green balloon is from Charlie he said that any colour at all would do

He whispered that the other day he sent his special red balloon to you too

The orange one is from Daddy I think he picked it as he is eating fruit to lose some weight

Inside he has sent you a big daddy squeeze to arrive today at Heaven's gate

Which colour balloon did Mummy pick she chose her balloon at the very start

Mummy picked the yellow one because it's cheerful and gladdens her heart

Nanny sent the pink balloon to match the ribbons in your hair

She wants you to know that to her, you are with her everywhere

Granddad picked the blue balloon he likes that colour very much

He isn't very good with words so it is filled with feathers for you to touch

The red balloon is the biggest that is because carefully wrapped inside

Is all our love and kisses and the tears that we have all cried

The ninth balloon is light blue and this one is from your Mummy too

She said just one balloon was not enough to send all her love to you

----

To My Dad

It did not seem to me that such a lot that I was asking for
For you stay for just a while and I would never ask for more
But now my heart is aching and life seems so unfair
I cannot imagine going on knowing you are not there
How can I face the future without you by my side
If my love could have healed you, you never would have died
I didn't foresee this day would come when we would have to
say goodbye
For our hearts had beat in unison bonded so close were you
and I
If my heart was divided into sections, the biggest piece has
gone with you
But others here hold the little bits and will help to see me
through
Whatever life now has in store for me I know that we will
meet up again
For without believing that is true my heart will forever hold
this pain

Today I thought I would send you an email as I am guessing in this day and age
Heaven must have computers to record the angels work alphabetically on each page
I would like to write to you whenever I think of you and tell you how we are all coping
I have to admit I will need to write often and so I was wondering well more hoping
That when you receive my emails would it be possible to somehow send me a reply
Don't worry sis I haven't gone mad, just send a sign like a twinkling star up in the sky
I miss you as soon as I wake and all day long my heart has this emptiness like a dull pain
I find myself reliving things we did together I want more time to spend with you again
When the sun comes out I think of you when the wind blows I think I hear you call
It is snowing now is it your tears mingled with mine I cannot stop crying today at all
Yesterday I realised I will never get a birthday or Christmas card again or a phone text
So, I went through my cupboard and after a bit of looking I know exactly what I'll do next
I found my last cards from you so I have put them in my memory box safely stored away

You see now next year I can get them out on those occasions
and to myself I can say
I received a card from you and I have read the words that you
wrote from your heart
Then I can send cards to you via heaven's email words to keep
us joined though apart

Yesterday I brought a blue Rose that I will plant in our garden here on earth for you

When they come out in flower they will be beautiful and remind me of a love so true

So, each morning I can say hello to you and every evening I will whisper goodnight

Though I will take you with me everywhere in my heart though you are out of sight

When as surely as night follows day, the petals will fall as the seasons come and go

I will not be sad as they will bloom again in spring for my love will help them grow

I hope you can see that blue rose its new growth nestled up against your garden chair

If I close my eyes I imagine you too are remembering all we shared that is my prayer

Yesterday I know you saw me weeping so many memories that bring you to my mind

A photo or the words in a song, some days are easier others are not or so I find

Time helps or so people say but there is one thing I do know to be so true

Is that no morning dawns or night time falls without a thought my love of you

----

I still cannot bear as yet to think of you my friend as not living
Tomorrow I want to say goodnight I'm not ready for goodbye
In time I will smile at the memories we were blessed to share
Until then I will send my love to your home beyond the sky
We talked often of what we had learned from our life's journeys
Yet we never talked of how we would be as friends who were apart
We thought we had more time to talk, to laugh and to cry together
Sadly, that is not to be but I have our last meeting nestled in my heart
As we get older, I think we find it harder to move on from pain and loss
We think that we have time on our side and yet that time was not to be
Tomorrow I know you will be watching over your family as they say goodbye
You left this earth so very loved by the many whose lives you touched including me

----

Yesterday I am ashamed to say I tried to bargain with God
when I saw a homeless man begging on the street
Of course I cared as I looked into his despairing sunken eyes
and saw the worn out shoes upon his feet
But I thought about the safe haven he could live in if you took
him home to live dear lord with you
I thought you could send my sister back home as I know
miracles can happen and I just need one or two
I know that I should never pray for something that is classed
as being selfish or for personal gain
But I just wanted our family to be okay and for all our world
to be free from this loss and pain
I'm sorry lord that I decided that this man's life was mine to
decide I am so sorry that I know the tears I cry
Are for whoever he was before life took him to that street
corner, can you forgive me and I promise you that I
Have learnt that you and you alone decide and I was so wrong
but I have learnt another lesson today
If you hear me though I sinned can you give us the strength to
cope with our grief and teach me along the way
That we each have different feelings about how we cope what
we pray for and will take away from days like this
One thing we all share in and are united in is the everlasting
love we were blessed to share as we say goodbye to our dear
sis

I Will Be There

On the days when the road ahead seems just too far for you to
go
Turn around I will be there we will walk it together and take
it slow
On the days like today when small trips tire you out quite a
bit
Turn around I will be there we will find a quiet place to sit
On the nights when though weary you just cannot escape in
sleep
Turn around I will be there and it is okay when fearful if at
times we weep
On the days when I nag you as to whether you have taken
every pill
Turn around I will be there it's my way of coping because you
are so ill
On the days when I'm so busy I know you think that I don't
care
Turn around I will be there it's just some thoughts I cannot
share
On the days when you are uncertain of just what lies ahead
Turn around I will be there let's be unsure together instead
On any day or night do not think I am too busy to be who you
need me to be
Turn around I will be there we will take every step of this
journey together you and me

In my hand I am holding a present that I brought for you with all the love that I have in my heart

For reasons that no longer matter you never saw it nor the inscribed words, to read when we were apart

At the centre of my gift is a candle every time I pass it I wonder if perhaps I should light the flame

I decided to keep it as it is instead in my mind I will light a candle in your memory every time I say your name

So far since you have left us I have lit so many candles the skies are lit up in every corner of the land

I miss you yesterday, today, tomorrow and forever wish for just one more day to hold your hand

----

I prayed last night that I would dream of you, it was not to be so I made up a dream instead

I revisited the day we did the "Round Robin" trip together it was a beautiful image in my head

We had done the trip and were now in town, do you remember Angie how cold it was that day?

We brought some cards in our favourite shop and in the bakers we laughed as you made Malcolm pay

We did all the charity shops on our way back, your lovely man was still cringing at the cost

My dream fades here for a moment, I cannot see through the tears I cry for what we all have lost

You are back with me now and we are in your home where you cared so well for all who came to your door

I see you clearly in every room but my heart breaks for I know such a day as this can be no more

On Saturday all of us who loved you so were in the heart of your home, your daughter got us there together

If love and our tears could have healed you, you would be safe at home with us now and live on forever

My images fade and I must have slept when I awaken just for a few precious moments I forget

Please walk beside us and guide our way precious sister as none of us are ready to say our goodbyes just yet

----

You only have one life but if you live it to the fullest it is enough

Some days are easy to get through other days can be tough

Start each day with a smile and you will find folk will smile at you

Start the day with a grimace and you will end it feeling sad and blue

Love cannot be purchased in a shop it is something that lies within

It is in each and every one of us you just open the door and invite it in

It's a wonderful possession for it has the ability to increase in value day by day

If you find it has visited you in any form welcome it and nurture it so it is here to stay

----

Today I have posted your Christmas card addressed simply with your name and Heaven's Gate

I wish you could tell me that it has arrived, here on earth post is erratic I don't want it to be late

It is a different type of card this year for none of the printed verses said what I needed to say

So, you will find that inside the card is blank except for those words that I tell you every single day

Every night before I sleep I pray that you feel the love and loss of all those you have left behind

I know that rarely a single day passes by when a thought of you is never far from my mind

If it should snow, I will say you are wrapping your loved ones in a blanket made with all your love

If it rains, I will say that you are crying along with us for one more hug that reaches down from Heaven above

If the wind blows, I will say be still and listen for your message is there to be heard on the gentle breeze

If as surely as night follows day, this year know how surrounded you are by our love this Christmas please

----

Night Duty

Here I sit at half past three
Now there's only you and me
No bells have rung for quite a while
So, I told a joke to make you smile
But then it got quite out of hand
You laughed so much you couldn't stand
We had gone upstairs now to room five
For now, the bells they were alive
I looked at you, and you at me
You laughed again and then we'll see
You left the room at quite a pace
Down the stairs I heard you race
I followed you down, I called out "Sue"
Then I realised you were in the loo
I knocked the door and asked if you were okay
From inside I thought that I heard you say
Oh, I've laughed and laughed till I nearly cried
Now I've a pain running right down my side
No more jokes not another one tonight
Or the ladies here will think we're not right
I heard the chain flush and slide back the door
One look at your face and I laughed no more
"Not one word" you said "about organs and vicars"
I have laughed so much I have wet my knickers

Every morning as a new day dawns I think of you and each evening the same as I watch the beauty of a sunset

As I and others go about the daily routine of living, please do not think that even for a moment I forget

Yesterday when I smiled in passing at a neighbour and to their question answered "I am fine and yes I am okay"

Sometimes I think today I am alright and other times I cannot imagine what got me through another day

So many reminders, sometimes a song on the radio, the scent of a flower or a similar smelling perfume

I find myself closing my eyes and hoping when I open them you will be there as you were in my living room

I still look at my phone and wish somehow as if by magic I could receive just one more text message from you

Your voice is on the answer phone, even after all this time I cannot delete it, you would tell me that it is something I must do

Whether we believe in a life after this earthly one or not, forever do we know so we are born and so we die

It is the timing and the fact that without warning, how do we who are left behind get the chance to properly say goodbye

I bargained with God the other day I am ashamed now that I felt the homeless man may have been better off not living

Would anyone really miss him as much as we do you, I was wrong I am sorry I hope you will be forgiving

When we grieve we forget that at times others may be suffering too in different ways that we cannot see or understand

Today I am back where I like to be caring for others and willing always to offer a shoulder to cry on or just a helping hand

----

Where did this dreadful illness come from that you see in your mirror hanging on the wall

This sickness that now makes decisions for you as to whether you are too big or too small

Unbidden it takes over your whole being the way you think, look and the way you feel

It decides during the day that you must starve yourself, yet from the fridge at night you steal

There is help and support readily available for the sufferer yet they rarely seek it you will find

Though by now so ill they feel they must be in control, to their loved ones this seems so unkind

There is very little help for the sufferers' families who have limited or no guidance in just what to do

For a Mum this is especially difficult because it is the love in her heart that rules in her care for you

You discover quickly that love alone is not enough to drive this destructive illness away from your door

For though at times you seem to have made progress, setbacks and heartache come quickly to the fore

The sufferer will never have meant to hurt you they tell you that they didn't choose to be this way

But a mum thinks why would you worry me like this I know I have voiced it more than once before today

Illogically you feel that they should just stop it, eat normally so the family mealtimes can be as they were before

But logic plays no part in this disease and your heart grieves because the happy family is no more

You try different tactics, you stop nagging them, you don't ask constantly what they have eaten today

You give them your trust to be in control, but at night just in case earnestly for it to stop do you pray

The professionals warn you that the sufferer will be devious, for example they will eat a meal and your heart is so glad

Whilst you are rejoicing at the progress they are making behind closed doors they quietly dispose of the food they have had

If the illness wasn't so very distressing, you could almost liken it to some kind of game

The sufferer needs to be always in charge, when you push them you become someone to blame

I have lived with this for exactly two years now, everything I have tried has turned out so wrong

In private I'm tormented because my child is so unhappy but I cannot do this anymore I am just not that strong

For you see though I have made my child so sad I have, in my pushing her to get well, I have destroyed our family

Now everyday responsibilities all seem too much I want someone else to take over and remove this fear from me

The thing I've learnt most from this journey is that with Anorexia sufferer's honesty doesn't pay

Because if you tell them that you are unhappy they will accuse you of ruining their day

You see you cannot hurt as you are not the poor victim they are the one who is suffering not you

If you show weakness they see you as selfish it is something as a caring Mum surely you would not do

Now you look at all the years of your so-called mothering
being so blessed so proud of all that she would achieve
To come to this as a family now so dysfunctional with no end
in sight and you cannot make it okay all you can do is to grieve

----

The Ballet Dancer

Tomorrow is your birthday I cannot believe that this year you
will be ten

Mummy could not think what to send you, she could not
decide and then

She thought back to when she was your age and what she had
liked to do

Without another thought she knew exactly what present she
would send to you

Inside the parcel delivered to Heaven's door you will find a
ballet outfit in the palest blue

It is the exact same colour as she had so it gladdens her heart
to imagine you in one too

Your brothers have picked their own gifts they have each
chosen what they wished to send

Bradley has sent a blue ribbon for your hair and a forever
teddy that says he will always be your brother and your friend

George has sent you some ballet pumps they are black but are
covered in lots of shiny glitter

Charlie has sent you a blue basket filled with sweets inside
and a note that says please pick up your litter

He thinks that when things blow down from the sky everyone
in Heaven is playing outside

He asked Mummy if you have a school in heaven and a park
with swings and a big slide

Daddy has sent you a locket you must wear it close to your
heart each and every day

Inside is a tiny picture of your family so you never feel that we are too far away

Nanny went to your resting place and she left you some beautiful flowers they are white and also pink

She writes you lots of poems she says it helps her to feel close to you especially at this time of year I think

Grandad is doing lots of work in the garden he is making areas all different and made out of wood

If we your three brothers get to play out there in the summer I wish you will come and join us if you could

Mummy has sent you one other gift it is a blue box and it is tied up with a big blue bow

She has filled it with at least a million kisses, the box is now quite heavy for a little girl you know

We all miss you Chloe every day not just on your birthday and we love you more than words can ever say

Please don't forget to send us all a sign on the breeze that you love us all too and that you are okay x

----

Today as I sat opposite you in the cafe, though you chattered away you looked sad

I wanted somehow to tell you that I understood all the fears that you had

All those other people around us eating, talking, enjoying the things that they shared

You didn't look any different to anyone else because no one looked properly or cared

But perhaps in my judgement of others I am maybe being a little unkind

Because they cannot see your illness for they cannot see inside your mind

If I had not travelled the same pathway as you sadly are walking today

I too would not have looked at you properly or really listened to what you wanted to say

The healing will come from yourself and I hope your struggles are very soon at an end

Although I cannot make your world right I will always be ready to listen as your friend

----

Martyrdom

Do you ever sit and wonder or feel at times that life's unfair

When Lady Luck has visited and once again your name wasn't there

Do you accept your lot quietly and never dream of making a fuss

Even though it seems it is always you who again just missed the bus

Do you struggle three steps forward yet still seem to slip back two

No matter just how hard you try why does nothing goes right for you

Are you ever heard to mutter, "Well, hopefully someone else is getting a rest."

Whilst the world and his wife are on my back but I can survive this new test

But now and then when you are feeling down and yet another thing has gone wrong

It is sometimes really difficult for you to see your way forward to carry on

So many people seem to need you and often all in completely different ways

So again you get a hold on yourself and decide it's just one of those days

You try so hard to stay cheerful and pretend that you really don't mind

But now and then self-pity creeps in and you do feel that life is unkind

You know that you only get out of life what you give and you are trying your best

So why is life this continuous struggle more than for him, her and the rest

You have tried to live by a little motto that you would always if you could, do good

But sometimes it does seem so futile and you do wonder just why you should

----

As today is your birthday I thought I would write you a little verse

I will not need to put my signature as it is from your favourite arse

I don't know how many lines I will write they will probably only fill a page

For lately I have been preoccupied with trying to guess your age

At first I thought I would put thirty-nine but I feel I am being too kind

So, I decided to settle for forty-one and I hope that you don't mind

As today is a special day I will let you indulge and have some fun

But remember your good intentions and refuse that last sticky bun

Sincerely though "Happy Birthday" I hope your day is good and free from tension

Just make sure you are back by Monday so you can go and collect your pension

----